3-D Printing

by Hal Marcovitz

NORWOOD HOUSE PRESS

Cover: A 3-D printer on display at the 3-D printing fair in Erfurt, Germany.

Norwood House Press
P.O. Box 316598
Chicago, Illinois 60631

For information regarding Norwood House Press, please visit our website at:
www.norwoodhousepress.com or call 866-565-2900.

PHOTO CREDITS: Cover: © epa european pressphoto agency b.v./Alamy; © Alexander Kharchenko/Dreamstime.com, 11; © AP Images/John Locher, 20;
© AP Images/Marcio Jose Sanchez, 19; © Barcroft Media/Getty Images, 17; © Belekekin/Shutterstock.com, 30, 41;
© Bloomberg via Getty Images, 9; © BSIP/Getty Images, 39; © Business Wire /Getty Images, 8; © Daniel Garcia/Getty Images, 36;
© Ethan Miller/Getty Images, 26; © Fernando Blanco Calzada/Shutterstock.com, 16; © Jim West/Alamy, 34; © John Bowling/Alamy, 29; © Luis
Robayo/AFP/Getty Images, 38; © Moreno Soppelsa/Dreamstime.com, 6, 24; © Patrick T. Fallon/Bloomberg via Getty Images, 32; © Piero Cruciatti/
Alamy, 14; © Scanrail/Dreamstime.com, 5

Hardcover ISBN: 978-1-59953-759-7
Paperback ISBN: 978-1-60357-867-7

LIBRARY OF CONGRESS CATALOGING-IN-PUBLICATION DATA

Marcovitz, Hal, author.
  3-D printing / by Hal Marcovitz.
    pages cm
  Includes bibliographical references and index.
  Summary: "Describes the invention and development of 3-D Printing. Explores
trials and tribulations along with the technological advances seen today. Includes glossary, websites, and bibliography for further reading"-- Provided by
publisher.
  Audience: Age 8-12.
  Audience: Grade 4 to 6.
  ISBN 978-1-59953-759-7 (library edition : alk. paper) -- ISBN 978-1-60357-872-1
(ebook)
  1. Three-dimensional printing--Juvenile literature. I. Title.
  TS171.95.M37 2016
  621.9'88--dc23
                                                              2015027485

313R—012018
Manufactured in the United States of America in North Mankato, Minnesota.

CONTENTS

Note: Words that are **bolded** in the text are defined in the glossary.

CHAPTER 1

A New Way to Make Things

Since the era of the **Industrial Revolution**, most things are made the same way—on assembly lines. In this method, a product moves down a conveyor belt from station to station. Workers put the product together as it moves by. Workers each have a station where they may bolt, glue, weld, or sew one piece of a product to another. This process is used for a variety of products, from toys to cars. In some cases a product may need just a handful of pieces to make it whole, such as a toy. In other cases, such as cars, thousands of parts must be put together. Today parts of a product are often made in different cities or countries. Then they are shipped to a factory where the assembly is finished.

In the 1980s another way to make products was developed. It uses the 3-D printing process. In 3-D printing, a product is designed on a computer. The software lets the designer make a 3-D image of the product. All sides, angles, and curves of the object can be made and seen on the computer screen. They can be seen in any view the designer needs: top, bottom, side to side, and so forth. When the designer is done fashioning the product, it can be made on a 3-D printer. Christopher Barnatt is a computing and future studies professor at Nottingham University in Great Britain. He says, "Within a decade or so, it is likely that a fair proportion of our new

Designers use computer software to create a 3-D image. Once complete, the image is transmitted to a 3-D printer where the final 3-dimensional product is rendered.

possessions will be printed on demand in a local factory, in a retail outlet, or on a personal 3-D printer in our own home.

Printing Layers

Today most people own a computer printer. A printer uses ink to make words or images on paper. These come to the printer from the computer. 3-D printers do not use ink and paper. They use things like plastics, metals, ceramics, and glass. They may even use some foods, such as chocolate. These are applied in liquid, molten, or powdered form through a **nozzle**. The printer builds the object layer by layer, from bottom to top. "When most people hear about 3-D printing, their mind leaps to their old, familiar desktop printer," writes Cornell University robotics professor Hod

Substances are distributed through the nozzle to build objects layer by layer.

Lipson and technology journalist Melba Kurman. "The biggest difference between an inkjet printer and a 3-D printer is one of dimension. A desktop printer prints in two dimensions, spraying colored ink onto flat paper documents. A 3-D printer fabricates [makes] three-dimensional objects that you can hold in your hand."

The credit for the 3-D printing process does not go to just one inventor. During the 1980s many experts worked on the idea. One early effort was developed in 1983 by Chuck Hull of Valencia, California. He came up with the process known as stereolithography. In this process, liquid layers of plastic or other materials are applied one on top of another. Then they are hardened to make a 3-D object. Another breakthrough took place in 1986 in the computer lab at the University of Texas by a student, Carl Deckard. He came up with a process called selective laser sintering (SLS). In SLS, materials are laid down in powders. Then they are heated into solid forms. Since the first versions of 3-D printing were developed, other methods have emerged as well. But all 3-D processes are similar. An object is made inside a printer, bottom to top, layer on layer.

DID YOU KNOW? ?

Chuck Hull, the inventor of stereolithography, was inducted into the National Inventors Hall of Fame in 2014.

Stereolithography and Selective Laser Sintering

Chuck Hull named his 3-D printing process stereolithography because it combines two familiar concepts to make objects. Lithography is a form of 2-D art that dates back to the 18th century. It uses ink that is applied to a flat and moist surface that has been treated with grease. The grease absorbs the ink. But the moist and ungreased areas repel the ink. Through this process, an image known as a lithograph emerges. The term *stereo* is familiar to music fans. People play their music on stereos. But the term has its roots in a Greek word that means "solid." Since it builds a solid by applying layers to a flat surface, much as a lithographer applies ink, Hull named the process stereolithography.

As for how selective laser sintering (SLS) earned its name, the term *sinter* means to compact a mass into a solid form through the use of heat. In this case the heat comes from a laser, which puts out a very hot beam of light. The high temperature is made because the laser process excites atoms, typically argon. This high heat turns the powdered material into a hard mass. A computer directs the laser and selects the shape of the object that is made through the SLS process.

3-D Systems' Selective Laser Sintering (SLS) technology enables designers to build micro-detailed parts and features.

Environmentally Friendly

3-D printing is also known as additive manufacturing. The additives are the raw substances that are fed into the printer. A 3-D printer uses plastics, ceramics, or metals in a way similar to how a regular printer uses ink. Most things are made out of huge supplies of materials. These are cut using die cutters. Or they may be cast using liquid or molten materials poured into molds. To make a small metal picture frame, a huge piece of sheet metal is fed into a die cutter that makes hundreds of frames at a time. A picture frame can also be made with liquid metal that is poured into a mold of the frame, then cooled until it hardens.

Either way, the metal that is left over is usually thrown out or the waste metal may

Silica sand is the base material for making 3-D printing molds.

be gathered up and trucked to a recycling plant. There it is melted down and recast into a reusable form. The new material is then trucked back to the picture frame company to be used again. With additive printing, no waste is made. Every ounce of material, whether it is plastic, metal, or chocolate that comes out of the nozzle, is used to make the object.

DID YOU KNOW?

3-D printing may hold great promise. But at this point the market for 3-D printers is still growing. Sales estimates from 2013 were 56,500 reaching to 5.6 million in 2019.

method is not friendly to the environment. Waste that is not recycled may be buried in a landfill or burned. Since a 3-D printer uses all the material fed into it, there is no waste. Joris Peels is a technology writer. He says, "As a process, 3-D printing has several . . . advantages that make it more environmentally friendly than mass production. . . . By using less material because it is an additive process we harm the earth less in creating things."

The use of all the material to make the object is what makes 3-D printing different. In conventional manufacturing, raw materials are removed to produce the object and the excess is thrown away or recycled. This type of manufacturing is called **subtractive**. Unfortunately, this

3-D Printing in the Home

For years 3-D printers cost hundreds of thousands of dollars. Only large companies could afford to use them and they were mostly used to make pieces of a product, not the entire thing. In recent years printer manufacturers have been able to make desktop 3-D printers for home use. These can cost less than $1000. This lets many people design and make a number of items for their homes. Barnatt says that as more companies start making 3-D printers, this will help reduce the prices. He thinks that within the next decade, 3-D printers made for home use will cost no more than $500.

People who own 3-D printers find they can design and make many things. Parents can make Christmas ornaments with an image of their child's face. Golfers can print their own golf tees with their names pressed into the sides. People can make their own coffee mugs with favorite sayings or images on them.

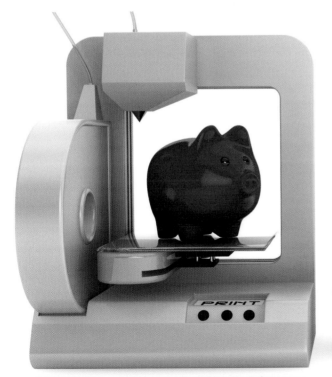

A home 3-D printer can produce many everyday products, such as multi-colored piggy banks.

2-D and 3-D

All 2-D, or two-dimensional, shapes share three features. They all have length, breadth (also known as width), and area. When laid out on paper, a rectangle's longest side is its length. The rectangle's shorter sides are its breadth. The inside is its area. Of course, other objects can be made in 2-D: letters of the alphabet as well as drawings and photos, for example. But all 2-D objects have a length, breadth, and area.

All 3-D, or three-dimensional, objects also share features. They are all solid. They all have length. They all have height. This is the measure of the object from bottom to top. All 3-D objects have depth. This is the thickness of the object. A common 3-D object is a cube. A cube has six sides, all equal in length and height. When all six sides are formed to make the cube, the depth is equal from side to side and top to bottom.

A shelf needed to fit a certain space in a home can be custom printed. Musicians can print their own guitars in any colors or shape they like. "Like all great periods of industrial transition, the 3-D printing revolution will be driven forward both by what individuals want to do as well as by what we all more collectively need to do. The things we want to do may well involve personal fabrication at home," says Barnatt.

In the near future, 3-D printers may be found in many more homes. The items made on 3-D printers, such as ornaments and coffee mugs, will be made by creative people who have mastered 3-D printing.

CHAPTER 2

The 3-D Culture Emerges

In the 2012 thriller *Skyfall*, villains blow up James Bond's Aston Martin sports car. But the film's producers did not blow up a real Aston Martin. It is a very expensive car. It costs around $300,000. Instead, for the film, a one-third sized model of the car was blown up on camera. The model was made with a 3-D printer. The use of a 3-D model in the making of a movie shows how 3-D printing has been accepted as a new, efficient, and inexpensive way to make things.

There are many examples of how 3-D printing is becoming a common part of life. Some can be found in Paris, New York, and other fashion capitals. Each year fashion models strut the runways to show off the latest designs from the world's top designers. In more and more cases, those clothes are not designed in sketchbooks and made with fabric, needle, and thread. Rather, they are made on 3-D printers. Even swimsuits have been made through 3-D printing. Nadir Gordon is an Argentine designer. In 2015 she unveiled a

This piece of clothing was made on a 3-D printer.

woman's swimsuit made with 3-D printing. "I began to study the vast world of 3D printing and became fascinated by it, seeing it as an opportunity to create garments and accessories in an innovative [new] way," says Gordon.

CAD Design

Making clothes, swimsuits, a model of a sports car, or any other items on 3-D printers requires knowledge of CAD. That stands for computer-aided design. First the design is done on the computer. Then it is sent to the 3-D printer, which makes the product. There are many CAD programs for designers, just like there are many

Fashion and 3-D Printing

Many of the world's top clothing designers are turning to 3-D printing. They use it to make special clothes, such as prom gowns and party dresses. Most clothes are made of fabrics, but not clothes made on 3-D printers. Fabrics such as cotton or wool cannot be melted or made into powder or liquid. So they cannot be ejected from the nozzle of a 3-D printer. Fashion designers must use melted plastic to make their clothes.

Designers who use CAD design their clothes in separate shapes such as triangles. Then they arrange the shapes on their computer screens to form a dress. The dress is then printed with a very thin strand of plastic that has the feel of fabric. Designers can even print buttons and loops right into the clothes, without needing to sew them on later.

Designers can also ensure the dress is a perfect fit. The body of the model or customer can be scanned with CAD software. This means the designer has the exact dimensions he or she needs to ensure the dress fits just right.

programs to produce text on a computer or improve photos taken with cameras or smart phones.

CAD has changed the way designers work. Before CAD, they drew their projects by hand on graph paper. They used tools such as mechanical pencils, T-squares, rulers, triangles, and French curves. John Herrman is a technology writer for *Popular Mechanics*. He says, "CAD modeling . . . has changed what it means to be an engineer and

CAD software allows designers to create sophisticated 3-D images.

revolutionized everything from toy design to aviation."

Plenty of people use CAD and 3-D printing to find new and better ways to make products that are normally mass-produced in factories. Walter Holemans is an engineer. He also loves boating. He races the double-hulled sailing vessels known as catamarans. As the catamaran skims across the top of the water, the skipper pilots the boat with a submerged rudder.

Holemans found his boat's wooden rudder was grainy and increased drag in the water. This slowed down the catamaran. So he designed his own rudder, which he made on a 3-D printer. The new rudder had less drag. This made the boat go faster. Impressed with the results, Holemans took the plan a step further. He made an entire 8-foot (2.4m) catamaran on a 3-D printer. "I realized I could . . . print parts that would be impossible to [create on a] machine," says Holemans.

Hybrid Manufacturing

Many large companies have come to the same conclusion as Holemans. Some have made their products on assembly lines for decades, but they have started using 3-D printing instead. Some companies, like Ford Motor Company, are using 3-D printers to make prototypes of parts. A prototype is a part used in a test phase of a product. Most cars have thousands of parts. Before ordering thousands or even millions of parts mass-produced, companies run tests on them using prototypes. Before using 3-D printers to make its prototypes, Ford made each test part with molds or die cutters. Now, if the 3-D printed prototype works, Ford then orders the part to be mass-produced.

Car tires made entirely of paper on a 3-D printer.

Other companies do more than just use 3-D printed parts as prototypes. They actually use parts made on 3-D printers in their final products. These companies use 3-D printing to make tiny parts that may not be recognizable to consumers. These parts include gears, disks, elbows, wheels, and other parts that fit into products that are still made on assembly lines. In 2012 the business journal *Forbes* said that some $3-billion-worth of products per year are made at least in part through 3-D printing. The number of products is expected to increase greatly in the future.

Using 3-D printing to make some parts of a product is known as hybrid manufacturing. Some parts are made through 3-D printing but others are still made with molds or die cutters. GE Aviation makes aircraft. It uses 3-D printing to make many parts for its jet engines, but the entire engine is not 3-D printed. Steve Rengers is director of research and development for the company. He says, "Because you're doing something one layer at a time, you can essentially build in elaborate passages into your product. It opens up design freedoms. . . . You're able to produce designs and components that you could never do with traditional manufacturing."

3-D Printing Aboard the Space Station

3-D printing has even been done in space. In September 2014 NASA put a 3-D printer in the cargo that it sent to the International Space Station (ISS). The ISS is home to hundreds of mechanical and electronic devices. If one of them stops working, the right tool to make the repair may not be available.

In the past it may have taken months before the next cargo shipment would arrive with the specific tool needed by the astronauts. In November 2014 astronauts

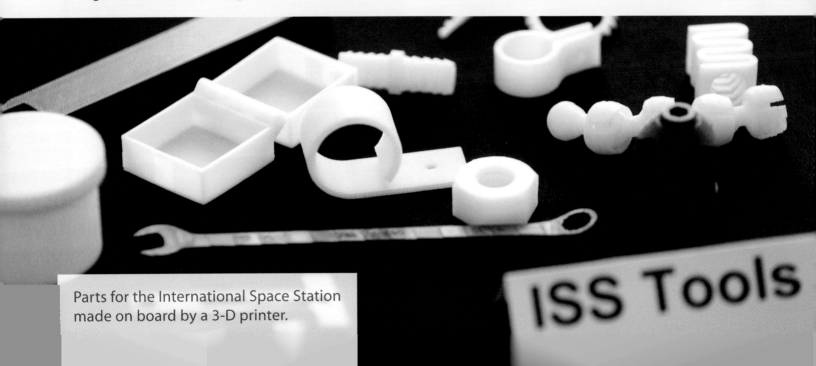

Parts for the International Space Station made on board by a 3-D printer.

ISS Tools

3-D Printing with Chocolate

It is no secret that chocolate can be melted into a gooey mess. The Hershey Company is one of the world's largest makers of chocolate candies. It uses 3-D printing to make customized candy for people. The company's 3-D printer is named the CocoJet. It can make custom-designed candies in dark, milk, or white chocolate. Hershey unveiled the CocoJet in 2015 at Hershey's Chocolate World. This is the company's megastore in its home city of Hershey, Pennsylvania.

The CocoJet works like any 3-D printer. A design is made on a computer. Then it is sent to the CocoJet. The melted chocolate comes out of the nozzle. The nozzle is guided by the printer into the custom shape. Hershey executives say the CocoJet can be used in bakeries to make customized candies for special occasions such as birthdays. They say caterers can use CocoJets at weddings so that personalized candies can be made for the bride and groom and their guests.

A 3-D food printer displays a design in chocolate on a piece of bread

aboard the ISS asked for a wrench of a certain size. A CAD designer on the ground designed the wrench and e-mailed the plan to the ISS. There it was made on the 3-D printer.

The printer was made by Made In Space. This is a Mountain View, California company. It makes 3-D printers for spacecrafts. The ISS printer has special features that let it work in zero gravity. For example, as the additive comes out of the nozzle, it is held by a sticky substance. Aaron Kemmer is the CEO of Made In Space. He says that since the 1960s, when the era of manned spaceflight began, nothing had ever been manufactured outside of Earth. Now, he says, a tool has been made by astronauts in orbit. "In 2014, we've taken [a] significant

DID YOU KNOW?

Made In Space is the company that made the 3-D printer for the ISS. It is trying out an additive that has the texture of lunar soil. The company says that if its experiments work, astronauts on a moon base may be able to use lunar soil for their 3-D printing needs.

step forward," he says. "We've started operating a machine that will lead us to continual manufacturing in space."

It is clear that 3-D printing is changing the way things are made. America and other countries plan to step up their space programs. New missions are planned in

Making the Past Come Alive

Museums have found ways to use 3-D printing to help their exhibits come to life. CAD designers made a 3-D printed version of a prehistoric whale fossil. It went on display in 2014 at the National Museum of Natural History. This museum is in Washington, DC. In Kenya scientists found parts of skulls of prehistoric humans. Complete versions of the skulls were made using 3-D printing. This gives people a vision of the heads of humans who lived 1.9 million years ago. These 3-D printed models are on display at the National Museums of Kenya. 3-D printers have made a life-like model of Abraham Lincoln based on photos and paintings of him. It is on display at the Smithsonian Institution in Washington, DC.

the future for the moon and Mars, and 3-D printing could very well play a large role in those missions. 3-D printing has been used to make new fashions, rudders for catamarans, parts for jet engines, and a wrench for use on the ISS. All of these show how 3-D printing can be used to change the culture of manufacturing in today's society.

CHAPTER 3

The Maker Community

Today's computers for home use are very powerful. This means they can drive the type of high-tech software needed to run CAD programs. Amateur crafters who want to design their own creations have bought the software and learned how to use it. These crafters are members of an informal "maker community." To make their crafts, they use 3-D printers that are now available for consumers.

Home-based 3-D printing uses a process that was developed in 1988. It is known as fused deposition modeling, or FDM. In FDM, the additive is fed into the printer in a thin plastic strand. This strand is known as a filament. It is heated into molten form as it comes out of the nozzle. This makes it soft and flexible. (The term *fused deposition* comes from fusing, or melting, the filament, also known as the deposit, into an object.)

FDM was invented by Scott Crump. He is an engineer from Eden Prairie, Minnesota. Crump thought of the idea while making a toy frog for his two-year-old daughter. To make the frog, he used

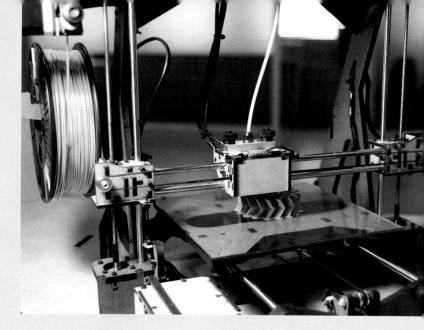

FDM can be used as an additive. Once heated into a molten form, it becomes soft and flexible and easily flows through the nozzle.

a hot-glue gun that he filled with candle wax and polyethylene, both in their liquid states. (Polyethylene is a plastic, most commonly used for grocery bags.) As he made the frog with the hot glue gun, layer by layer, Crump wondered whether he could build a machine to do the same task.

The RepRap Project

Crump designed the machine and soon founded a company named Stratasys to make the devices. These machines are large and costly. They are meant for industrial use rather than home use. But in

2009 three young makers, Adam Mayer, Zach Smith, and Bre Pettis, founded a new company in Brooklyn, New York. It is called MakerBot Industries. The company is one of the first to make desktop 3-D printers for home use that use the FDM process.

MakerBot had its roots in the RepRap Project. This is an international effort to make cheaper 3-D printers for the maker community. (*RepRap* stands for "replicating rapid prototype.") Engineers who worked on the project swapped ideas over the Internet. They worked under the "open source" concept. This means their ideas were shared. And everyone had free rein to use the ideas or improve them. When most people come up with an idea, they like to keep the plans to themselves. They may fear others will steal their designs. But the RepRap participants were more interested in making 3-D printing widely available to consumers.

Bre Pettis and *Margo*

Bre Pettis was born in 1972. He worked as an assistant in film production and as an art teacher. He partnered with Adam Mayer and Zach Smith to form MakerBot in 2009. He stepped down as the head of MakerBot in late 2014. But he still works to advance 3-D technology.

Pettis now heads a project known as Bold Machines. It aims to use 3-D technology for new purposes. One of Bold Machines' first projects was to use 3-D printers to make the characters for the animated film *Margo*. The title character, Margo, is a detective. Her parents vanish while on a space mission. The film follows Margo and other characters as they explore the cosmos in search of Margo's missing parents.

MakerBot is an inexpensive 3-D printer used in the maker community.

The first printers made by Maker-Bot had many problems. Through the open source concept, the company got a lot of help and it was able to make many improvements. By 2012 many home-based makers were using the company's printers.

Plant Holders, Chess Pieces, and Coffee Mugs

Today members of the maker community have access to desktop 3-D printers. They have started making things no one had ever thought of before. Colleen Jordan

Millennials Are Makers

Part of the reason 3-D printing is becoming popular is due to the lack of hands-on skills training given to the millennial generation. This is people born in the 1980s and later. Many schools have been forced to cut shop and home economics classes. These classes taught skills such as car repair and cooking. Many people today grew up in homes where both parents worked, meaning the parents were often too busy to teach their kids "do it yourself" skills.

Many people have turned to the World Wide Web. They watch videos that help them learn how to use tools, cook, and design things for their homes. They visit online communities to share their ideas and showcase and sell their handiwork. Many of their creations are made on 3-D printers. By 2015 the website Etsy, for example, had more than 1 million members who exhibit and sell their crafts. Each year several cities host Maker Faires. There amateur crafters show off and sell their creations. Each year about 500,000 people attend Maker Faires in America.

lives in Atlanta, Georgia. She has designed plant holders that attach to bicycle parts. This lets riders bike with their favorite houseplants on board. She has also designed and printed jewelry that holds tiny plants. Customized smart phone cases are popular among makers. People design their cases in all colors. They may include their names, images of loved ones, imprints of their kids' hands, or other features that have special meaning to them.

One maker is Joshua Pearce of Houghton, Michigan. He says he is so dedicated to 3-D printing that he hardly shops for consumer goods. Instead, he makes them himself. He has made chess pieces, shoes, tape dispensers, and mugs. For inspiration, he strolls through Walmart stores and scans the shelves to look for products to make at home. "I take great pleasure, and my wife teases me about it, walking through Walmart and saying, 'I could print that, I could print that,'" Pearce says.

Pearce often makes things he could easily buy in a store, but he says a real plus of 3-D printing is that people can make things they are unable to buy or that are customized to their own taste. A factory making thousands of smart phone cases per day cannot stop the conveyor belt to customize each case. Makers using 3-D printers can add special colors, images, or their initials or names. "Anything that is remotely customizable, 3-D printing is going to win out," says Pearce. "You can do fantastic things."

With 3-D printing available, many everyday objects can be made from home.

Making a Gun on a 3-D Printer

In some cases what comes out of a 3-D printer may not be accepted by others as a good use of the technology. In Texas, political activist Cody Wilson was in the news in 2013. He made a handgun on a 3-D printer. This worried law enforcement officials.

Most states have strict laws about how people can get a gun. Would-be gun owners have to submit background checks to make sure they do not have a criminal record. Also, most states require stores that sell guns to keep records of their sales. That way, if a gun is used in a crime, the store's records can help police trace the gun to the owner.

When Wilson made a gun with a 3-D printer, there was cause for concern. If somebody wants to rob a store, now all he or she has to do is make a gun at home on a 3-D printer. Chris Murphy is a US senator from Connecticut. He says, "If somebody can just print a gun off on a 3-D printer in their basement, it effectively renders our firearms laws meaningless. You'd never have to go through a background check to

There is large concern regarding printing guns on 3-D printers.

get a gun if you can just go over to your buddy's house and print one off."

Jonathan Rowley is director of design for Digits2Widgets. This is a London-based 3-D printing and design company. He says printing guns on home 3-D printers may not be practical. The would-be robber would have to be very skilled in CAD, and with many moving parts, a gun would be a complex CAD project. It would require the skills of an expert CAD professional. "It's simply a lot easier for crooks to get hold of a gun the old-fashioned way, buying them or stealing them, than to fuss over a 3-D printer for a couple of days, only to end up with a warped plastic blob or, even worse, something that blows up in their hands," he says.

DID YOU KNOW?

The filament used in FDM includes the chemical polylactic acid. It is made from corn. This is why many makers say their 3-D printers often smell like bakery ovens.

The US Congress responded to the threat of 3-D printed guns. It extended a ban on plastic firearms that was due to end in 2013. The ban was needed because guns made out of plastic cannot be easily detected by X-ray machines or metal detectors at airports. Under law, guns may not be carried onto airplanes.

The controversy over the use of a 3-D printer to make a gun continues, but it

3-D Junk

Makers have come up with some creative designs for household items. But some makers still have a lot to learn. That is what technology writer Elizabeth Royte thinks. She wonders whether the wide availability of 3-D printers will lead to the production of mountains of junk.

She first asked this question in 2013 after she toured the headquarters of 3D Systems in Rock Hill, South Carolina. The company makes 3-D printers. 3D Systems was founded by Chuck Hull. Royte went to a demonstration of the company's first printer made for home use. The printer is called the Cube. "Just because any-body's ideas can take shape doesn't necessarily mean they should," she says. "I saw shelf after shelf of what some people try very hard not to describe as cheap plastic [junk]: brightly colored miniature vases, phone cases, jewelry, dolls and . . . skulls."

3D Systems unveiled their home 3-D printer, the Cube, in 2013.

has not stalled the maker movement. Each day, makers come up with new and creative projects. Their plant holders, jewelry, chess pieces, and coffee mugs are not mass-produced in factories. Rather, each item is a personal reflection of the time and effort makers devote to their craft.

CHAPTER 4

The Future of 3-D Printing

As 3-D printing moves into the next generation, experts see it being used to make even bigger projects. Entire houses have already been made through additive manufacturing. Each room in the house is made on a 3-D printer. Then the rooms are trucked to the construction site and assembled into the finished home. Based on that concept, even bigger structures are planned. In Amsterdam, Holland, architects Hans Vermeulen and Hedwig Heinsman are heading a project. They plan to build a four-story building that would be entirely 3-D printed. "We all know that 3-D printing is going to play a big role in the future," says Heinsman.

Research is under way to make cars entirely through the 3-D printing process. In 2015 the Phoenix, Arizona company Local Motors unveiled a new car. It has two seats and is electric-powered. It is named the Strati. It was made on a 3-D printer in 44 hours. Using CAD, designers combined the thousands of parts found in the typical car into a handful of printable objects. These were then easily assembled. "A 3-D printed car like ours will only have dozens of components," says James Earle, an employee of Local Motors.

Local Motors is already planning to build 3-D printing centers to make the cars. The first center is planned for suburban Washington, DC. If 3-D technology continues to advance and people are able to buy more sophisticated 3-D printers, they may be able to make their own cars on their own 3-D printers.

Local Motors' Strati, the world's first 3-D-printed car.

Local Motors says it intends to keep an open source policy for the designs of its cars. It has made the plans available on its website so anybody can download the plans for the Strati. If they have a 3-D printer, they can make a Strati in their own garage.

The day may come when people can print their own cars at home. If so, it would be something of an ironic twist in the history of car making. The concept of using mass production to make cars was born in 1913 when Henry Ford introduced an assembly line to make the Model T Ford. Before founding his car company, Ford built his first car in his garage, piece by piece. In the future, people may print their own cars in their own garages.

Improving Lives of the Disabled

3-D printing holds a lot of promise when it comes to improving the lives of the disabled. It is already providing surgeons with new tools to repair injured

DID YOU KNOW?

In 2012 the US government set up the National Additive Manufacturing Innovation Institute. It is in Youngstown, Ohio. It works to help industries find ways to use 3-D printing. It also tries out new techniques and materials used in 3-D printing.

Cool Prosthetics

The typical prosthetic limb can cost as much as $70,000 when it is made in the usual way. This involves pouring liquid plastics or metals into molds. Some pieces are die cut. Kids who need prosthetic limbs often need them replaced many times as they grow. At Washington University in St. Louis, Missouri, CAD designers make prosthetic limbs on 3-D printers at costs of about $200.

For years people who have been forced to wear prosthetic limbs have taken great pains to hide them. The limbs can look strange. They may have steel rods and hinges or other mechanical parts. People who have been fitted with prosthetics made on 3-D printers work with CAD designers to personalize their new limbs and make them as attractive as possible. Sydney Kendall of Chesterfield, Missouri, lost her right arm below the elbow in a boating accident when she was six years old. Seven years later, in 2014, Sydney was fitted with a prosthetic arm at Washington University. CAD designers printed the arm in pink. Sydney had asked for that color. On her first day back at school after getting her new arm, Sydney says her classmates liked her new prosthetic. She says, "They were like, 'Sydney, you're so cool! You're going to be famous!'"

A set of prosthetic hands made from a 3-D printer.

or deformed bodies. With the help of a 3-D printer, in 2015 Boston surgeon John Meara rebuilt the skull of a two-year-old Oregon girl named Violet Pietrok. She had been born with a severe birth defect. Her eyes were on the sides of her head, not in the front of her face. This left the girl nearly blind. To fix Violet's eyes, Meara operated on her skull to move her bones into new places.

Before the operation, Meara had images made of Violet's skull that showed the deformed bones. Using those images, a CAD designer made four 3-D printed copies of Violet's skull. Meara then practiced the operation on the 3-D printed copies. This let him see which bones had to be moved into new places. "This isn't like free throw practice," Meara says. "You can't just go out and try and if you miss, try again. 3-D printing is a way to let you see where you're going. For example, we wanted to move the eyes closer together and we can see where there might be problems. This way, we can just do it again in practice rather than having it have to be right the first time." When he was operating on Violet's skull, Meara kept a 3-D model nearby so he could compare the girl's skull to the model as he worked.

As Violet grows older she will need more surgeries to continue to correct her skull. In the meantime, though, her parents say she is doing well. Her father, Matt Pietrok says, "She's handled this all so well. She's amazing. . . . We just love her little face. I don't even notice the differences she has anymore."

A prosthetic leg made from a 3-D printer.

Replacing Limbs

3-D printing is also being used to replace missing or damaged limbs. CAD designers have made **prosthetic** limbs for patients born without arms or legs or who have lost limbs due to accidents. Richard Van As is a South African woodworker. He lost most of a hand in a sawing accident. He used the Internet to connect with American CAD designer Ivan Owen. Owen designed a new prosthetic hand for Van As. The South African man's new hand works with the motion of his wrist. After designing the prosthetic hand, Owen sent the design over the Internet to Van As, who took the design to a 3-D printing company where it was made.

Sometimes, body parts do not have to be replaced but may still need more

3-D Printing and Dentistry

People who have severe tooth decay or break their teeth in accidents often have to be fitted with crowns. A crown is a new top for the tooth. The dentist files away the severe decay or the broken portion, then makes a mold of a new tooth by pressing wax into the remaining portion of the tooth. The next step is for the dentist to send the mold to a lab. There it is made into a crown. The crown is returned to the dentist and then fitted into the patient's mouth. The process can take several days or weeks and, of course, two visits to the dentist's office by the patient.

Some dentists now make new crowns on 3-D printers while their patients wait. In 2014 Saul Kaplan says he watched in amazement as his dentist, after removing the damaged part of his tooth, inserted a tiny digital camera into his mouth to photograph the tooth. The image was then sent to a computer. The dentist used a CAD program to design a crown. The dentist used a 3-D printer to make the crown. Then he fit the crown into Kaplan's mouth. The entire process, Kaplan says, took no more than ten minutes.

A dental technician uses a CAD system to design and produce a dental prosthesis.

support. At Children's Hospital in Oakland, California, experts are developing new braces for young people with deformed spines. The old, typical braces are bulky and uncomfortable. They must be strapped on tightly and worn during all waking hours. A new 3-D printed version looks like an old-style woman's **corset**, but it is made of very thin materials and form fitted to each patient. Wearers say it is very comfortable.

For patients who are completely incapacitated, CAD designers are developing **exoskeletons**. Patients who could benefit from exoskeletons are those who cannot rise from their wheelchairs. The full-body suits are skintight and custom designed to fit the patients. They are made on 3-D printers. They are made of light yet strong materials. The suits have motors that help the users move their legs and arms. The suits give mobility to these patients, enabling them to slowly move about on their own. Amanda Boxtel lost the use of her legs in a 1992 skiing accident. In 2013 she was fitted with a 3-D printed exoskeleton. Now she can walk on her own. "It was made from me and for me," says Boxtel. "I want to think of it as my sleek and sexy sports car."

New Body Parts

The next advance in medical 3-D printing will be to print new body parts with **human tissue**. Body parts may be printed with combinations of human tissue and plastics or other materials. Through 3-D printing, experts at Princeton University in New Jersey have made a human ear. They used human tissue and silicone. This is a rubber-like substance that is often used in plastic surgery. The ear is more than just **cosmetic**. It has wire coils that send electrical impulses to the brain. This means it can give the sense of hearing to a hearing-impaired person. 3-D printing can also make new skin for cancer patients who

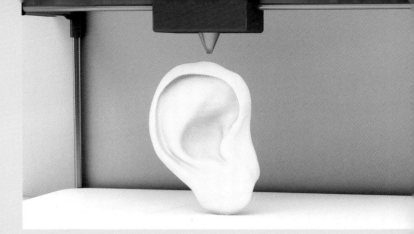

A 3-D printed ear includes a wire coil that sends electrical impulses to the brain.

have lost tissue. Scientists can make tissue like new ears or new skin because they have been able to grow cells in lab dishes for years. They start with **stem cells** from patients. These cells can be fed through the nozzle of a 3-D printer in the same way plastics or metals are used to make flower pots or smart phone covers. Experts think that soon, entire human organs can be made through additive manufacturing.

The first steps have already been taken. In 2013 a two-year-old Illinois girl born without a **trachea** received a new organ made on a 3-D printer. It was made of tissue grown from her stem cells. "This is an exciting new area of medicine. It has the potential for being a very important breakthrough," says Dr. Jorge Rakela. He works at the Mayo Clinic in Phoenix, Arizona. He says, "3-D printing allows you to be closer to what is happening in real life."

Revolutionizing Human Society

At this point, 3-D printing limits amateur makers to small projects. These include flower pots for their bikes, smart phone covers, or coffee mugs with favorite sayings or photos. Industry is still in the beginning stages of using 3-D printing. Most products are still made on assembly lines. This uses a subtractive process and it adds to the waste that is piled up on the planet. Only when industries fully grasp additive manufacturing will all that waste stop. People like Vermeulen and Heinsman, car designers like those at Local Motors, and medical pioneers who are finding ways to make prosthetics or actual human tissue through 3-D printing keep working on it. Their efforts show the potential 3-D printing holds for changing human society.

corset (KOR-set): Also known as a girdle, a corset is a woman's very tight undergarment that extends from below the chest to the hips. Corsets were popular in the seventeenth and eighteenth centuries.

cosmetic (kos-MEH-tik): The properties of an object or person that provide the appearance of beauty.

exoskeleton (EKS-oh-SKELL-uh-tin): A bone-like support found on the outside, rather than inside, the body. Insects have exoskeletons.

human tissue (HYOO-man TISH-ooh): The mass of cells that form the basic material of the human body, such as skin, or the physical properties of organs, such as the walls of the heart.

Industrial Revolution (in-DUS-tree-uhl rehv-oh-LOO-shun): The era of human civilization roughly from the late 18th century to early 20th century in which engines powered by steam, oil, and coal replaced manual labor, leading to an explosive growth in the ability to manufacture goods.

prosthetic (pros-THET-ik): An artificial limb or other part of the body.

nozzle (NAH-zul): A short tube used to direct the flow of a liquid or semi-liquid substance.

stem cells (stem sells): Cells that have not yet taken on specific characteristics, such as those that compose blood; scientists can guide stem cells to grow into specific types of cells, such as new skin cells for cancer patients.

subtractive (sub-TRAK-tiv): A manufacturing process in which raw materials are removed to make the product, such as metal cut away by a die cutter.

trachea (TRAY-kee-uh): The tube in the body that funnels air from the throat to the lungs.

Books

Carla Diana, *LEO the Maker Prince: Journeys in 3D Printing*. Sebastopol, CA: Maker Media, 2013. Carla wants to be an artist when she grows up but instead becomes an accountant. As an adult, she discovers 3-D printing and fulfills her desire to make art. The book is well illustrated with instructions on how 3-D printing is accomplished.

Maggie Murphy, *High-Tech DIY Projects with 3D Printing*. New York: PowerKIDS, 2014. An introduction to 3-D printing for young people, the book includes some easy-to-do projects. The author directs readers to online sources of CAD designs that can be downloaded and printed.

Terence O'Neill and Josh Williamson, *3D Printing: Makers as Innovators*. North Mankato, MN: Cherry Lake, 2013. A beginner's guide to 3-D printing, the book includes easy-to-follow instructions on CAD modeling. The book mostly covers 3-D printing with devices manufactured by MakerBot.

Chris Thorpe, *Adventures in 3D Printing and Design*. Hoboken, NJ: Wiley, 2015. A beginner's guide to CAD modeling and 3-D printing, the book provides nine projects for students to tackle.

R.H. Vissers, *I Am Printing 3D! Starting with 3D-Printing, Even If You Don't Own a 3D Printer*. Nuenen, Netherlands: BraveNewBooks, 2013. The author provides a history of 3-D printing, some easy-to-follow instructions on how to get started, and examples of finished projects. The book also explores future uses for the technology.

Websites

Bold Machines (www.boldmachines.com). The website is dedicated to the innovative projects underway by the program headed by Bre Pettis.

Visitors can find photographs of the 3-D printed characters for the film *Margo* and follow the progress of the film's production.

Maker Faire (www.makerfaire.com). This website lists the dates and cities where Maker Faires are scheduled. By following the link for Meet the Makers, visitors can see photos of many innovative projects, including those produced on 3-D printers, that have been made by amateur makers.

Thingiverse (www.thingiverse.com). Sponsored by MakerBot, Thingiverse features thousands of projects designed by amateur makers who have uploaded photos of their projects as well as the designs. Makers can download the designs for free and reproduce the projects on their own 3-D printers.

3DPrint.com (www.3dprint.com). The website serves as a news source reporting the latest developments in 3-D printing. Visitors can find news about manufacturers of 3-D printers as well as updates on interesting 3D projects that have been tackled by CAD designers.

"WUSTL Students 'Print' Pink Prosthetic Arm for Teen Girl" (http://news.wustl.edu/news /Pages/26901.aspx). The website tells the story of thirteen-year-old Sydney Kendall, who lost her arm in a boating accident. Sydney received a pink prosthetic arm at Washington University in St. Louis, Missouri, thanks to the efforts of CAD designers who produced the prosthesis on a 3-D printer.

INDEX

ABOUT THE AUTHOR

Hal Marcovitz is a former newspaper reporter and columnist. He has written more than 170 books for young readers. He makes his home in Chalfont, Pennsylvania. The author's daughter, Ashley Marcovitz, is a professional CAD designer.